Believe In Yourself

story and illustsrations by Will Slezak

ISBN: 978-1-7368205-0-6

CMN
NEWS
UNIC

In the big story today, an actual unicorn was found! The first ever in the existence of the world. WOW!...

You're probably wondering what bullying has to do with me? Well, first let me tell you a little story about a pony named Pokey.

Pokey was born very small, underweight and had a disfigured face. But Mommy and Daddy horse loved that baby pony no matter what!

Pokey got to play every day with Mommy and Daddy horse and it was fun, fun, fun!

Then one day Daddy horse came out and made an announcement.

It's time you go to school and learn what a horse must know. How to push, pull and plow, to help crops grow.

Mommy and Daddy horse brought Pokey to the horse stop, where all the ponies would gather for their journey to school.

Come on! This way!
They're about to leave!

On the ponies' journey to school, there was some bickering and snickering going on between them...

Wow, look at that funny-looking horse, that pony looks like it could be a pre-historic dinosaur!
Does it think it can be like one of us?
I don't think so!

Ya! Really!

Pokey and the other ponies finally reached horse school. Once there, some of the ponies said they had a "first day of school surprise" for Pokey.
WOW! that's awesome! Thanks, guys!

Pokey found out what the "first day of school surprise" was.

Pokey found out about lunch time.

and Pokey found out what happens after school too!

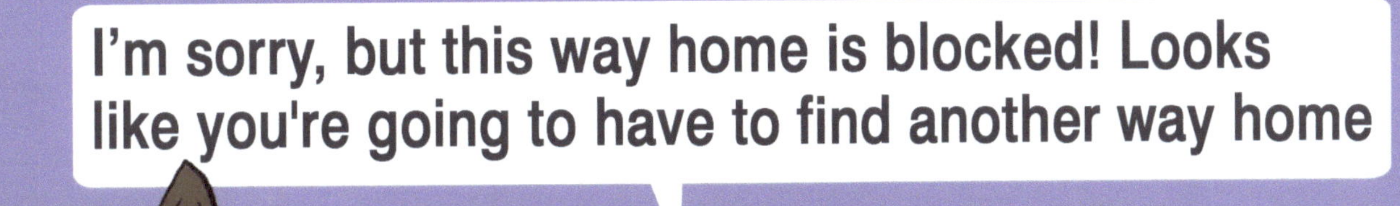

A few days later Momma horse found Pokey still in bed, not getting ready for school and asked why? Crying, Pokey answered...

I, I, I don't want to go to school! Everybody hates me! They all laugh and make fun of me! And call me an ugly looking dinosaur! Why are they so mean to me? What did I do to them?

You did nothing wrong! It's not right that they treat you like that! I know you don't want to get anyone in trouble, but the school principal must know about this, so that others don't suffer too! Daddy and I will have a talk with him as soon as possible!

Just then, as Pokey was looking out to the corral, a great sage blew in, and spoke...

Only through the winds of time will the real truth be shown. You must stay strong. Be you. And in the end, you will be the greatest!

Then, just as fast as he had blown in, he blew out.

The winds blow on and on with the passage of time...

Just two years later magic happened!

And guess who made national news?!

Just think how lucky the unicorn's friends are!
They'll probably be rich and famous too!

Wow!... Hey, do you think Pokey thinks of us as friends?

We learned a BIG lesson! We need to be friends with everybody! So in turn, they'll be friends with us.

I stayed strong. I believed in myself. Time passed, and I grew up into the real me. I showed them how great I really am!